The Butterfly Ballerina

The Interactive Healing Devotional for *ALL Women*

Written by Liberty Crouch
AN OVERCOMER SAVED BY THE GRACE OF GOD

Mission: To Proclaim Transformation and Truth
Publisher: Transformed Publishing, Cocoa, FL
Website: www.transformedpublishing.com
Email: transformedpublishing@gmail.com

A Gift From God

Presented To:

\---

From:

\---

Date:

\---

What is my goal as I complete this devotional?

_____
_____
_____
_____
_____
_____
_____
_____
_____
_____
_____
_____
_____
_____
_____
_____
_____
_____
_____
_____
_____
_____
_____
_____
_____

Table of Contents

Affirming Declarations

Acknowledgements

To know Mrs. INA Brown, is to know the fragrance of the beauty of the Holy Spirit; *The Proverbs 31 Woman.* Throughout this interactive healing devotional, Mrs. Ina Brown has left her imprint. Such passionate desire for women of every culture, to be made whole and the love of that desire which comes from the sacrificial love of Jesus Christ, was felt every time I met with her.

This woman of God, a selfless devout wife, with the anointing of a caretaker—so much love to give. A mother of many burdens unspoken, driven by the Hope of Glory to reconcile all that which was lost. Philanthropist—Kingdom seed planter and Kingdom builder, behind the scenes miracle worker, sister in Christ whom I simply admire for the patient endurance she models so eloquently, through every unspoken tear.

The Interactive Healing Devotional for All Women, the first of seven—*Butterfly Ballerina Devotionals,* is dedicated to the honor of Mrs. INA Brown; for her surrendered obedience to the Lord, taking time to meet with me even while she carried the burdens of her own life, in order for this devotional to be created as a tool to lead others to the One who heals, reconciles, restores, and redeems—for the healing of all women and to the Glory of God.

 Her teachings are filled with wisdom and kindness as loving instruction pours from her lips.

-Proverbs 31:26 TPT

About the Author

The Butterfly Ballerina was inspired by the Holy Spirit, during a time in my life when the trauma of my first marriage ended in divorce after only being married for a month or so. The man I married turned out to be an undercover binging alcoholic. I was a new believer in Christ and very passionate about the things of God, so this marriage was completely unevenly yoked. Much to my dismay, the state I resided in, has a law requiring couples to live separate for one year, before obtaining a divorce. But as God would have it, for the purpose of redemption, nothing is ever lost. The very date my divorce happened to be finalized was three years from the exact same day of my born again birthday.

My mom has always been extremely spontaneous. On my doorstep one day, I received a delivery. It was a box with a couple of gifts. Unbeknown to her, I would use these items to start my writing career. My first published work as an author was a non-fiction autobiography three part book series. I received the journal she sent at the same time I needed to express the pain I had endured. She also sent me blue butterfly wings, years later, near to the date of my divorce, as a symbolic reference to freedom. The same blue butterfly wings used in the images of this devotional and many other inspired pieces of my work as a digital fine artist.

A sister in Christ, whose family has been with me since the beginning of my walk in Christ, true worshippers indeed, celebrated this new freedom with me by going on a journey throughout western North Carolina taking snapshots of me as I danced with Father God, posturing in worship and praise to the One who Redeemed me.

I decided in my heart to surrender to God's will for my life, trusting Him to be everything He says He is in the Bible.

My passion comes from many wonderous encounters with the Lord and His faithfulness. There is one very specific posture of worship in particular as you read through this devotional you will notice—my hand reaching upward toward heaven and the other hand in front of my waist. This is the posture of dancing with Father God, in which the *Butterfly Ballerina* was originated, a story you will learn about in this devotional.

My hope is that I can reach you by sharing the words given to me through Divine love and mercy, to release healing by the power of the Holy Spirit, forever transforming you into who He created you to be.

✦

There is a 'Butterfly Ballerina' within you -

As you begin to trust God more and more, by giving Him your hand, you will see, He has been there waiting for you the whole time, with His righteous right hand outstretched from heaven to you.

Impartation

So do not fear, for I am with you;
do not be dismayed, for I am your God.
I will strengthen you and help you;
I will uphold you with my righteous right hand.
—Isaiah 41:10 NIV

Declare: "I surrender to His good and perfect will for my life."

This is a Love Story

The Divine Father who desires you,
His royal daughter;
to worship and love Him
to know His unconditional love
for you . . .
He is setting you free,
by calling you to dance with Him.

["]Bring all who claim me as their God,
for I have made them for my glory.
It was I who created them.'"
-Isaiah 43:7 NLT

Declare: "I surrender to His good and perfect will for my life."

> . . . I have chosen you
> and have not rejected you.
> -Isaiah 41:9 NIV

Declare: "I surrender to His good and perfect will for my life."

Purge rejection, hurt, bitterness,
disappointment, & your complaints here, in
order to receive His good & perfect will for your life.

_____

_____

_____

_____

_____

_____

_____

_____

_____

_____

_____

_____

_____

_____

_____

_____

_____

_____

_____

_____

_____

_____

_____

Commitment

But I will give my thanks
to you, Yahweh, for you
make everything right in
the end. I will sing my
highest praise to the God
of the Highest Place!
-Psalm 7:17 TPT

The next few pages are now the
making of _your_ New Story . . .
A commitment between you and the Lord.

Dear Heavenly Father,

I know my sins are forgiven because of Your finished work on the cross. I do ask that You wash me clean with the redeeming blood of Jesus Christ and continue to lead me daily in a disciplined life of repentance with You, through the conviction of the Holy Spirit and the grace to make the necessary changes.

I choose to live my life according to what pleases You, in that way, the Joy of my salvation will give me strength to endure and persevere through the trials and temptations that I face.

In my heart I choose to set Jesus Christ apart as holy and I acknowledge Him as my personal Lord and Savior.

I receive everything Jesus Christ already paid for on the cross for me, by faith.

Amen.

Great is the LORD!
He is most worthy of praise!
He is to be feared above all gods.
-1 Chronicles 16:25 NLT

Prophecy

**"My experience encounter with the Living God,
my testimony as an overcomer, will break
chains of bondage for generations to come."**

I will be surrendering to God's good and perfect will. I will be empowered by the uplifting affirmations and faith declarations. I will experience a new way of thinking, transformed into the way I was designed by God to think and live. These words were divinely created for me. God never makes a mistake. Therefore, I will put my confidence in the God who created me.

Jesus Christ gave His life for me, I accept Him, receive Him, and welcome Him into my heart and life not only as my Savior, but also my Lord. I know that without Him there is no atonement for my sins. The Scriptures tell me, "If we confess our sins, He is faithful and just to forgive us *our* sins and cleanse us from all unrighteousness" (1 John 1:9). So I do just that, by faith.

Jesus Christ already paid the price so that I can be healed. Although there are millions of women here on earth, I realize God created each woman to be unique. I am uniquely created by God on purpose. My flaws and imperfections are not greater than who God created me to be. The pains of *trauma, rejection, disappointment, fear, shame, emotional hurt, set back, sickness, disease, addiction, abandonment, betrayal* and everything else that could have crushed me, no longer have any power over me! The God who spoke light into existence, saying, "Let light shine from the darkness," (*see* 2 Corinthians 4:6) is the very One who sets our hearts ablaze to shed light on the knowledge of God's glory revealed in the face of Jesus, the Anointed One.

And they sang a new song, saying,
"Worthy are you to take the scroll
and to open its seals,
for you were slain, and by your blood you
ransomed people for God
from every tribe and language and
people and nation,
and you have made them a kingdom
and priests to our God,
and they shall reign on the earth."
-Revelation 5:9-10 ESV

The God who spoke light into existence, saying, "Let light shine from the darkness," is the very One who sets our hearts ablaze to shed light on the knowledge of God's glory revealed in the face of Jesus, the Anointed One.

But this beautiful treasure is contained in us—cracked pots made of earth and clay—so that the transcendent character of this power will be clearly seen as coming from God and not from us. We are cracked and chipped from our afflictions on all sides, but we are not crushed by them. We are bewildered at times, but we do not give in to despair. We are persecuted, but we have not been abandoned. We have been knocked down, but we are not destroyed. We always carry around in our bodies the reality of the brutal death and suffering of Jesus. As a result, His resurrection life rises and reveals its wondrous power in our bodies as well.

-2 Corinthians 4:6-10 VOICE

Declare: "I surrender to His good and perfect will for my life."

Your Response:

_____
_____
_____
_____
_____
_____
_____
_____
_____
_____
_____
_____
_____
_____
_____
_____
_____
_____
_____

Divinely Orchestrated

Dear Sister,

I don't believe in coincidences. I do believe that every-thing the enemy tries to harm us with, the Lord turns around and uses for His glory.

One day in particular, my vehicle needed some repairs (or so I thought). Before work, I dropped my car off at the repair shop and rode to work with a friend who agreed to meet me at the repair shop. After work I caught a ride with her and her two-year old daughter back to my car, which was parked across the street from a house of worship, (a place I regularly visited, to spend time with the Lord).

The praise music was so loud it caught both our atten-tion. We couldn't help but notice the worship service in progress across the street. My friend asked me if I want-ed to go inside with her. I said, **"Yes, let's go."** So, I got in my car, which by the way, was found to be in perfect working condition, and drove across the street to be closer to the place of worship. If I hadn't dropped the car off at the repair shop right across the street from the place of worship, I wouldn't have known the service was going on that night.

This was clearly Divinely Orchestrated!

But to each one of us grace has been given as Christ apportioned it. -Ephesians 4:7 NIV

Declare: "I surrender to His good and perfect will for my life."

As soon as my friend's two-year old little girl walked in the doors of that place, she ran to the altar and started dancing in the presence of the Lord. She was falling down and getting back up and twirling and laughing. As I watched her dance, I heard my Divine Father speak. He said, **"That's what it looks like."**

I finally understood what He meant. I watched more intently and my Father gave me a *vision*. He showed me a ballerina wearing a white dress, with her right arm extended toward heaven and her left arm wrapped around her waist, as if she were holding on. This ballerina was dancing on a white music box. The vision I received *is* the cover of this book.

I knew that this was the undefiled expression of dance He was calling me to. My Father said, *"That ballerina is you, my daughter. Reach for My hand and I will hold you up. Trust Me, dance with Me."* And so I did. And so will you!

Figuratively speaking, we all have a story to tell-we can choose to live and tell our story from one side of the street or the other. We can choose to stay at the repair shop and try to figure it out with our own strength **or** we can cross over to the other side of the street where Jesus is waiting, and by faith allow the God who saves our soul, who heals our body, and who gives us the same Spirit that resurrected Jesus Christ from death, to empower us with abundant life here on earth to live victoriously and prosperous.

The Love of God that is in you, will overflow and manifest healing. There will be healing even in your shadow as you pass by, others will be healed. Just like God did with Peter the Apostle in the Bible. As your faith walk with God the Father increases, so will your love overflow for others.
Read Acts 5:15-16

Declare: "I surrender to His good and perfect will for my life."

"I surrender to His good and perfect will for my life."

Your Turn

**Within these pages are space and opportunity
for you to write your new story.**

After this devotional has been completed, you can take your notes,
the revelation knowledge the Lord will have imparted to you, the miracles
of healing that you will have experienced; and publish your own book for
the glory of God to use *you* to reach other women,
through your overcoming testimonies.

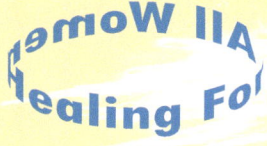

**Whenever you see this symbol,
let it remind you of the healing
that is your inheritance, and
the healing in your shadow**.

*Go and heal others in the name of Jesus Christ.
Yes, even now, in your weakness, brokenness, & even loneliness.
Christ is made strong within you.*

But he said to me, "My grace is sufficient
for you, for my power is made perfect in weakness."
Therefore I will boast all the more gladly about
my weaknesses, so that Christ's power may rest
on me. That is why, for Christ's sake, I delight
in weaknesses, in insults, in hardships, in
persecutions, in difficulties. For when
I am weak, then I am strong."
- 2 Corinthians 12:9-10 NIV

This healing devotional is for ALL women,
for every tribe, and language, and culture, and nation.

From the words of Jesus Christ to you:

... *"What do you want Me to do for you?"* ...
Read Mark 10:51-52

... *"Do you believe that I am able to do this?"* ...
Read Matthew 9:27-29

... *"Take heart, daughter,"* he said,
"your faith has healed you." ...
Read Matthew 9:22 NIV

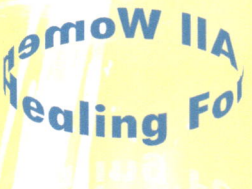

"The Spirit of the Lord is on me, because he has anointed me to proclaim good news to the poor. He has sent me to proclaim freedom for the prisoners and recovery of sight for the blind, to set the oppressed free, to proclaim the year of the Lord's favor." Then he rolled up the scroll, gave it back to the attendant and sat down. The eyes of everyone in the synagogue were fastened on him. He began by saying to them, "Today this scripture is fulfilled in your hearing."
- Luke 4:18-21 NIV

Your Response:

_____
_____
_____
_____
_____
_____
_____
_____
_____
_____
_____
_____
_____
_____
_____
_____
_____
_____
_____
_____
_____
_____
_____
_____
_____
_____

Love

L

O

The Love That Leads,
His Love With Wings

SURRENDER

V

E

I am ready to go on a new journey.
It starts with my Faith.
I am laying down all fears at the foot of the cross now and forever.
This is where my *true freedom* begins.

What is God saying to me?

"Submit to God and be at peace with him;
in this way prosperity will come to you.
Accept instruction from his mouth
and lay up his words in your heart.
-Job 22:21-22 NIV

From my darkest of days, to now,

Hope and new life

The dance of redemption

Holding onto my Father in heaven while

He leads me victoriously into His love

Renewed wings from His breath of resurrection

A new dance, a new song, a new outlook!

The love that leads His love

With wings - toward home

And we all, with unveiled face, beholding the glory of the Lord, are
being transformed into the same image from one degree of glory to
another. For this comes from the Lord who is the Spirit.

-2 Corinthians 3:18 ESV

Faith

**Building blocks of *Faith*
must start somewhere.
Let's create a foundation.
Search the Scriptures
to find your *Treasure*.**

For where your treasure is, there your heart will be also.
—Matthew 6:21

"I surrender to His good and perfect will for my life."

"Trust Me, I am not a man that I should lie.
People will let you down and hurt you, but I remain the same.
I am *Faithful* and *True*.
I love you with an *Everlasting Love*."
- *Your Father, God*

Trust is not built on
Forgiveness, but rather
Trust is built on Faithfulness . . .

. . . *"I have loved you with an everlasting love;*
I have drawn you with unfailing kindness.
I will build you up again,
and you, Virgin Israel, will be rebuilt.
Again you will take up your timbrels
and go out to dance with the joyful.
—Jeremiah 31:3-4 NIV

The Love That Leads,
HIS Love With Wings

God is not human, that he should lie,
not a human being, that he should change his mind.
Does he speak and then not act?
Does he promise and not fulfill?
-Numbers 23:19 NIV

He will be the sure foundation for your times,
a rich store of salvation and wisdom and knowledge;
the fear of the Lord is the key to this treasure.
-Isaiah 33:6 NIV

What is God saying to me?

Divine

Invitation

The Divine Father Who desires His Royal Daughter to Know His Unconditional Love for her, by setting her Free, through Calling her to Dance with HIM.

Reflect:

_____
_____
_____
_____
_____
_____
_____
_____
_____
_____
_____
_____
_____
_____

I am a Royal Daughter.
I am desired by my Divine Father.
I am loved unconditionally by Him.
My Father wants to set me free
from this world and its desires.
I am listening for my Father's voice.
One step at a time,
He will show me the Way.

So do not fear, for I am with you;
do not be dismayed, for I am
your God. I will strengthen you
and help you; I will uphold you
with my righteous right hand.
—Isaiah 41:10 NIV

"I surrender to His good and perfect will for my life."

DANCE WITH ME...

What are your first thoughts about this unknown journey ?

_____

_____

_____

_____

_____

_____

_____

_____

_____

_____

_____

_____

_____

> *He is the Rock, his works are perfect,*
> *and all his ways are just.*
> *A faithful God who does no wrong,*
> *upright and just is he.*
> *-Deuteronomy 32:4 NIV*

23

no Lord...

Because of the Lord's great love we are not consumed,
for his compassions never fail.
They are new every morning; great is your faithfulness.
-Lamentations 3:22-23 NIV

Ask yourself, "What would hold me back from a divine opportunity like this?

COME,
DANCE WITH ME...

*But the Lord is faithful,
and he will strengthen you and
protect you from the evil one.
-2 Thessalonians 3:3 NIV*

Why Not?

Is it shame, fear, guilt, rejection, condemnation?
What is holding you back? Take note of your thoughts and feelings,
do not let them sound louder than your Father's voice.

COME,
DANCE WITH ME...
MY DAUGHTER

Do not be afraid or discouraged, for the Lord will personally go ahead of you. He will be with you; he will neither fail you nor abandon you.
-Deuteronomy 31:8 NLT

Looking outward toward your future, what do you see?

Is it dark, foggy, bright, hopeful, or _____?

_____
_____
_____
_____
_____
_____
_____
_____
_____

no Lord...

In life, what are some of the setbacks, disappointments, emotional hurts, and traumas you have experienced?

These, along with doubt and uncertainty, may have contributed to your beliefs about Father God and your journey.

_____

_____

_____

_____

_____

_____

_____

_____

_____

_____

 *For I will restore health to you*
And heal you of your wounds, says the Lord, . . .
-Jeremiah 30:17

COME, DANCE WITH ME, DAUGHTER OF JUDAH, LET'S DANCE!

One step at a time, by faith, remember God, your Divine Father will help you on this journey to break free from all that holds you back. *Do you know that God calls you by name? He pursues you with relentless love. Will you now consider the possibilities? What is He calling you to do by faith?*

"Nations will see your righteousness and all kings, your glory. You will be given a new name that the Lord's mouth will announce. You will be a glorious crown in the Lord's hand, and a royal diadem in the palm of your God's hand.
-Isaiah 62:2-3 CSB

WHY DO YOU CALL ME LORD AND TELL ME , NO...

When we make Jesus Christ our Lord, we have made
Him the leader of our heart, mind, soul, and strength.
Will you now trust the God who created you to lead you into freedom?
How will you do it?

Trust in the Lord with all your heart
and lean not on your own understanding;
in all your ways submit to him,
and he will make your paths straight
-Proverbs 3:5-6 NIV

"Why do you call me Lord and then deny me?"

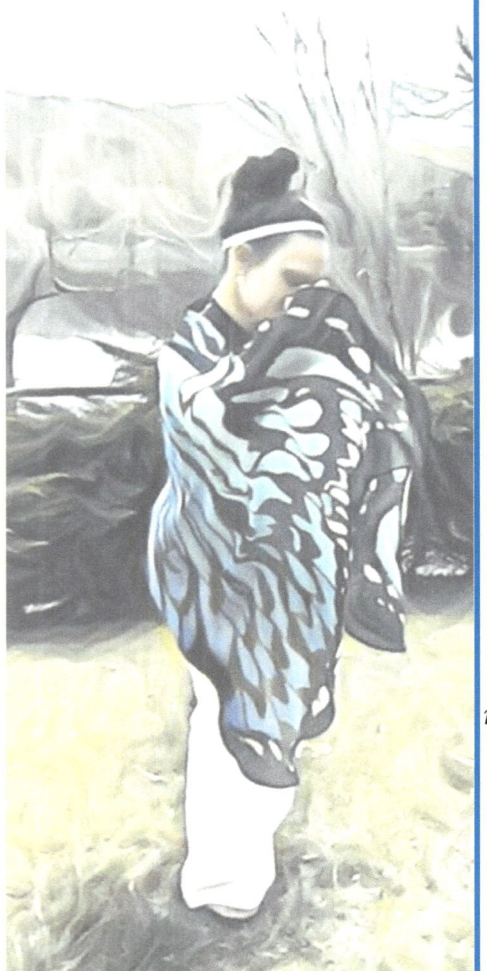

"I am confused, Lord. What does it even look like— dancing with You?"

My struggle with understanding my Father's request originated from a twisted version of what 'dance' meant to me. I was a professional exotic dancer from the age of eighteen through thirty. So, when My Divine Father asked me to dance, I couldn't comprehend what a pure and holy version of dance would look like.

Taking him by the right hand, he helped him up, and instantly the man's feet and ankles became strong. He jumped to his feet and began to walk. Then he went with them into the temple courts, walking and jumping, and praising God.
-Acts 3:7-8 NIV

Is there anything else holding you back from trusting Father God completely and dancing with Him on this journey called 'life'?
Remember to lay it down at the foot of the cross and reach up for your Father's divine hand.

The

Consideration

What does that even look like-Dance with You...?

Being vulnerable and transparent with God and yourself, is the *Key to Freedom's Gate*.

As you now consider reaching up toward heaven to take ahold of your Divine Father's outstretched arm – How do feel about it? What questions do you have for God?

Write your thoughts:

_____

_____

_____

_____

_____

_____

_____

_____

_____

But the wisdom that comes from heaven is first of all pure; then peace-loving, considerate, submissive, full of mercy and good fruit, impartial and sincere.
-James 3:17 NIV

The Conversation

The Lord is near to all who call upon Him,
To all who call upon Him in truth.
-Psalm 145:18

In a world where 'Christians' are held to a higher standard— yes, to the unbelievers, but also to an even greater level amongst other followers of Christ. Sometimes, to the point where shame is implemented if you confess you are sick or have come down with a disease or are going through depression, rather than laying hands on the sick so they can recover (see Mark 16:18 and James 5:14).

Have you ever experienced a church hurt? Are you ready to let go of any unforgiveness, bitterness, and emotional pain? Your past is your past, allow God to use it for His Glory. Remember to write your thoughts. You are on your way to freedom.

Spiritual pride, amongst other things, has hindered specific moves of the power of God in the church and around the world. I was so stuck in the place of darkness. I did not know who I could talk to without feeling *so* ashamed. I felt like I was not living up to *peoples'* definition of a Christian. Here I was, someone who already overcame so much, and who has faith for others to be healed, but not able to get to the very place that not too long ago I knew even existed.

Has the busyness of life taken you away from the place of your daily Jesus encounter—the place where Jesus speaks and releases healing? That is the place where trauma wounds are filled with the Dunamis Power of Christ Jesus' Resurrection and the soul is made excellent.

In parts of this healing devotional, I have shared a little bit of my life, in bite size segments of transparent rawness. I encourage you to be as honest, but with yourself and God. This journey will always start and end at the cross. The cross of Jesus Christ. This is where you encounter the Living God. This is where your healing will manifest. This is a safe place for you to have an opportunity for the next level of freedom and healing that you are destined to be a part of.

"Your level of honesty, determines your level of healing."
"My transparency is for your revival."

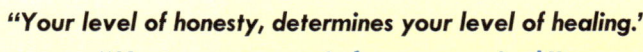

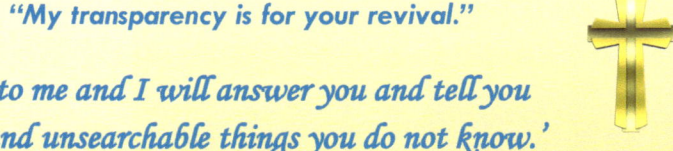

'Call to me and I will answer you and tell you great and unsearchable things you do not know.'
-Jeremiah 33:3 NIV

"I surrender to His good and perfect will for my life."

The Conversation

_____

_____

_____

_____

_____

_____

Let us then approach God's throne of grace with
confidence, so that we may receive mercy and find
grace to help us in our time of need.
-Hebrews 4:16 NIV

Some of the worst pains I've ever felt in my life, have been that of *betrayal*. It's an invisible mental terrorist to the extreme. Almost, as if its agenda was to break my spirit and leave me for dead, worthless in ministry, and not able to help others. The effects of this torment lasted longer than anyone in my trust circle would have expected, to say the least.

The pains of betrayal branched out into different forms of Post Traumatic Stress Disorder (PTSD), which stemmed from my early childhood and early adulthood. Abandonment and rejection caused inner soul wounds, also known as trauma. Suppressed emotional pain manifested into sickness in my body and left my mental health off balance. My attitude toward life in general was either off in fantasyland, a place of escape, secluded in isolation, or immobilized by *fear*.

Fears manifested in different ways. Worrying about things I had no control over, led to anxiety, and even panic attacks. My emotions were so unbalanced that on any given day, I would fall into *depression* and have sporadic crying episodes. All while putting on a smile to face the people I was entrusted to pray for, work with, and do everyday life with. All of this kept my true feelings and emotions suppressed and isolated.

I was fearful that someone would find out I was going through all of this. I could lose my job, my family wouldn't want to deal with me, my testimony as an overcomer would somehow be lost, and ultimately I would be *abandoned* – left to do life all by myself. This was all fear-based and caused by the lies I was believing. And there we have it, back to the original problem source – *abandonment*.

Does any of this sound familiar? Whether it's a church hurt, a family betrayal, the loss of a loved one, the loss of a job, unexpected loss of any kind, rejection, or abandonment, any hurt that is causing your healing to be delayed, must be identified. Please write your thoughts as Holy Spirit shows you.

Then you will call on me and come and pray to me,
and I will listen to you. You will seek me and find
me when you seek me with all your heart.
-Jeremiah 29:12-13 NIV

The Conversation

_____

_____

_____

_____

_____

_____

You've kept track of all my wandering and weeping. You've stored my many tears in Your bottle-not one will be lost. For they are all recorded in your book of remembrance.
-Psalm 56:8 TPT

The

Cares

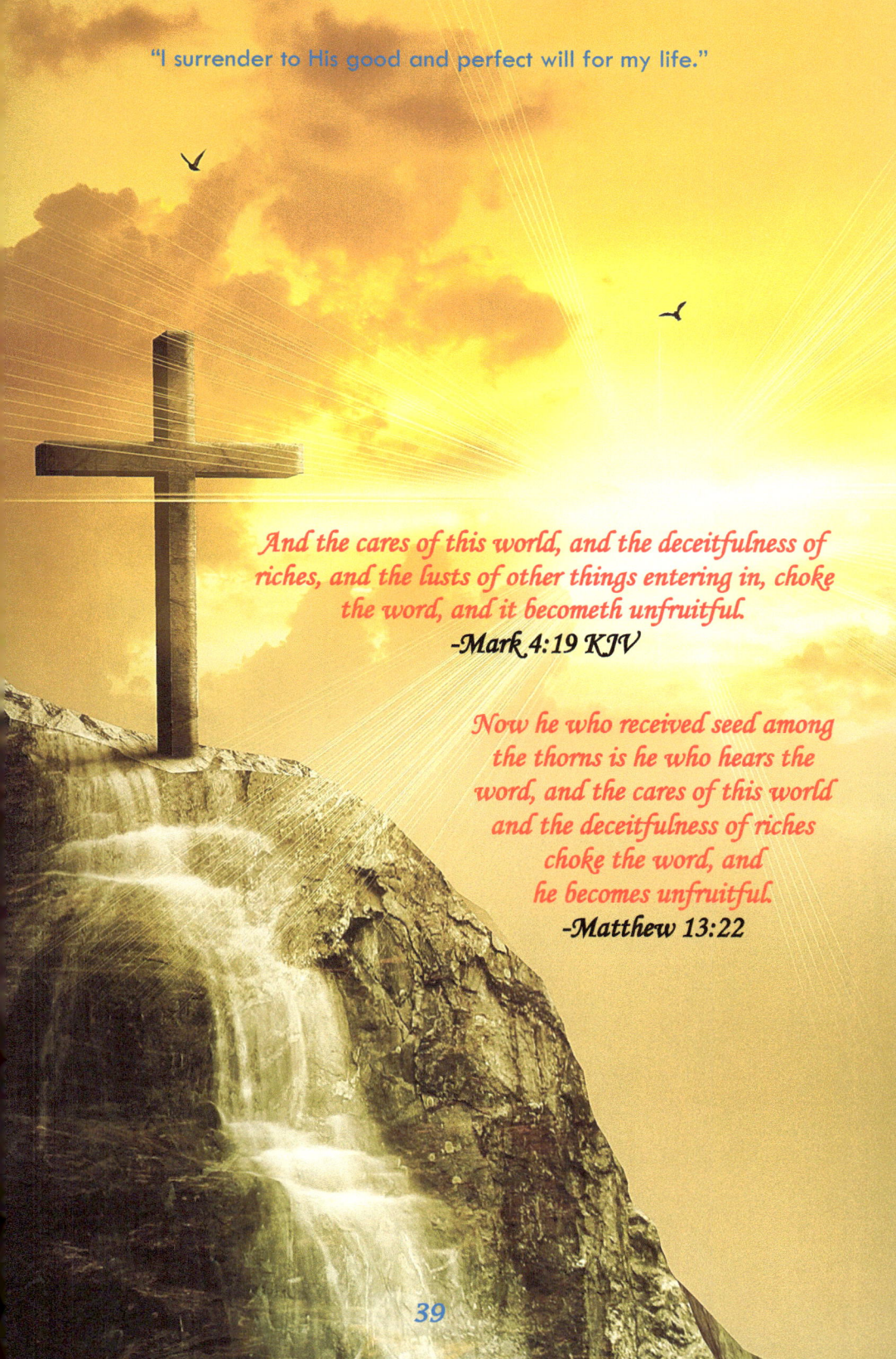

"I surrender to His good and perfect will for my life."

And the cares of this world, and the deceitfulness of riches, and the lusts of other things entering in, choke the word, and it becometh unfruitful.
-Mark 4:19 KJV

Now he who received seed among the thorns is he who hears the word, and the cares of this world and the deceitfulness of riches choke the word, and he becomes unfruitful.
-Matthew 13:22

"Cast your cares upon me, for I care about you," says the Lord.

Casting the whole of your care [all your anxieties, all your worries, all your concerns, once and for all] on Him, for He cares for you affectionately and cares about you watchfully.
-1 Peter 5:7 AMPC

But when you pray, go into your room, close the door and pray to your Father, who is unseen. Then your Father, who sees what is done in secret, will reward you.
-Matthew 6:6 NIV

"Cast your cares upon me,
for I care about you,"
says the Lord.

In my distress I called to the Lord;
I cried to my God for help.
From his temple he heard my voice;
my cry came before him, into his ears.
- Psalm 18:6 NIV

JESUS

Alabaster

Box

Luke 7:36-50 NIV
Jesus Anointed by a Sinful Woman

When one of the Pharisees invited Jesus to have dinner with him, he went to the Pharisee's house and reclined at the table. A woman in that town who lived a sinful life learned that Jesus was eating at the Pharisee's house, so she came there with an alabaster jar of perfume. As she stood behind him at his feet weeping, she began to wet his feet with her tears. Then she wiped them with her hair, kissed them and poured perfume on them.

When the Pharisee who had invited him saw this, he said to himself, "If this man were a prophet, he would know who is touching him and what kind of woman she is—that she is a sinner."

Jesus answered him, "Simon, I have something to tell you."

"Tell me, teacher," he said.

"Two people owed money to a certain moneylender. One owed him five hundred denarii, and the other fifty. Neither of them had the money to pay him back, so he forgave the debts of both. Now which of them will love him more?"

Simon replied, "I suppose the one who had the bigger debt forgiven."

"You have judged correctly," Jesus said.

Then he turned toward the woman and said to Simon, "Do you see this woman? I came into your house. You did not give me any water for my feet, but she wet my feet with her tears and wiped them with her hair. You did not give me a kiss, but this woman, from the time I entered, has not stopped kissing my feet. You did not put oil on my head, but she has poured perfume on my feet. Therefore, I tell you, her many sins have been forgiven—as her great love has shown. But whoever has been forgiven little loves little."

Then Jesus said to her, "Your sins are forgiven."

The other guests began to say among themselves, "Who is this who even forgives sins?"

Jesus said to the woman, "Your faith has saved you; go in peace."

All Women Healing Fo

*Share with God,
as He shares with you:*

_____
_____
_____
_____
_____
_____
_____
_____
_____
_____
_____
_____
_____
_____
_____
_____

We can learn how to overcome, in the Scriptures, through the examples of how others dealt with their personal struggles. But ultimately 'We Overcome' by the power that is in the shed blood of Jesus Christ. We are to walk in newness, new ways of thinking, as a result of receiving the mind of Christ.

We develop new perspectives when our hearts are transformed by the renewing of our minds. This takes place as the Scriptures become alive and active within us.

Men judge by outward appearance, but God looks at a person's thoughts and intentions (see 1 Samuel 16:7 MSG).

The alabaster box (or referred to as jar) is mentioned in three places in the Bible. Mary boldly approached Jesus and poured out her expensive perfume to anoint Him. Her action was looked down upon by fellow onlookers, however, it was greatly appreciated by Christ Himself.

*Don't copy the behavior and customs of this world, but let God transform you into a new person by changing the way you think. Then you will learn to know God's will for you, which is good and pleasing and perfect.
- Romans 12:2 NLT*

"I surrender to His good and perfect will for my life."

"Cast your cares upon me, for I care about you," says the Lord.

Casting the whole of your care [all your anxieties, all your worries, all your concerns, once and for all] on Him, for He cares for you affectionately and cares about you watchfully.
-1 Peter 5:7 AMPC

For the word of God is living and powerful, and sharper than any two-edged sword, piercing even to the division of soul and spirit, and of joints and marrow, and is a discerner of the thoughts and intents of the heart.
-Hebrews 4:12

The
Cross

"I surrender to His good and perfect will for my life."

From glory to glory ....

Mary overcame her shame by walking with Jesus.
Jesus healed her and accepted her.
Boldness was activated by approaching Jesus humbly,
and in sincere faith and love.

I AM EXCHANGING ALL OF MY SHAME NOW,
FOR BOLDNESS—AT THE FEET OF JESUS CHRIST.
MY LIFE IS MADE NEW MOMENT BY MOMENT
—GLORY TO GLORY.

Behold, you delight in truth in the inward being,
and you teach me wisdom in the secret heart.
-Psalm 51:6 ESV

"Cast your cares upon me, for I care about you," says the Lord.

Casting the whole of your care [all your anxieties, all your worries, all your concerns, once and for all] on Him, for He cares for you affectionately and cares about you watchfully.
-1 Peter 5:7 AMPC

Be anxious for nothing, but in everything by prayer and supplication, with thanksgiving, let your requests be made known to God; and the peace of God, which surpasses all understanding, will guard your hearts and minds through Christ Jesus.
-Philippians 4:6-7

Affirming
Declarations
Love, Courage, Faith, & Freedom

Kindness, Endurance, Compassion, Forgiveness, and Victory.

"Most of the time, the pain in a woman's heart is because of pain inflicted by another person, which lingers in our hearts while we hold on, suffering; allowing that pain to define us."—INA

"These are the key ingredients to being healed and finishing well, this Life of Freedom here on earth."—INA

Put on then, as God's chosen ones, holy and beloved, heartfelt compassion, kindness, humility, gentleness, and patience, bearing with one another and forgiving one another, if one has a grievance against another; as the Lord has forgiven you, so must you also do. And over all these put on love, *that is, the bond of perfection. And let the peace of Christ control your hearts, the peace into which you were also called in one body. And be thankful. Let the word of Christ dwell in you richly, as in all wisdom you teach and admonish one another, singing psalms, hymns, and spiritual songs with gratitude in your hearts to God. And whatever you do, in word or in deed, do everything in the name of the Lord Jesus, giving thanks to God the Father through him.*
-Colossians 3:12-17 NABRE

My courage is in the hand of my Father,
who leads me into His love.

Be strong and courageous.
Do not be afraid or terrified because of them, for the Lord your God
goes with you; he will never leave you nor forsake you.
-Deuteronomy 31:6 NIV

I am strong and courageous.
I am not afraid or terrified because of them,
for the Lord my God goes with me.
He will never leave me nor forsake me.

For God has not given us a spirit of fear,
but of power and of love and of a sound mind.
-2 Timothy 1:7

"I surrender to His good and perfect will for my life."

Courage, Freedom, & Faith

With child-like faith,
I will remain in obedience.

But whoever looks intently into the perfect law that gives freedom, and continues in it—not forgetting what they have heard, but doing it—they will be blessed in what they do.
-James 1:25 NIV

BELIEVE

It is God who arms me with strength,
And makes my way perfect.
–Psalm 18:32

I look intently into the
perfect law that gives
freedom, and I continue in it.
I do not forget what I have
heard, but I obey it and I am
blessed in what I do.

BELIEVE

Think only about the things in heaven, not the things on earth. Your old sinful self has died, and your new life is kept with Christ in God.
-Colossians 3:2-3 NCV

I am hidden with Christ in God.

The Interactive Healing Devotional for All Women

BELIEVE

[I]f My people who are called by My name will humble themselves, and pray and seek My face, and turn from their wicked ways, then I will hear from heaven, and will forgive their sin and heal their land.
-2 Chronicles 7:14

I think about the things that are in heaven, not of the earth. Things above and not below. I do not focus on my circumstances or the pains of my past. My thoughts are fixed on what God says is true because my old life died in Christ and I now live in the present moment, with God in my new life

"I surrender to His good and perfect will for my life."

BELIEVE

So we have come to know and to believe the love that God has for us. God is love, and whoever abides in love abides in God, and God abides in him. By this is love perfected with us, so that we may have confidence for the day of judgment, because as he is so also are we in this world. There is no fear in love, but perfect love casts out fear. For fear has to do with punishment, and whoever fears has not been perfected in love. We love because he first loved us.
—1 John 4:16-19 ESV

I abide in His everlasting love.

BELIEVE

Through the Lord's mercies we are not consumed, because His compassions fail not. They are new every morning; Great is Your faithfulness.
—Lamentations 3:22-23 NKJV

I have come to know and believe the love that God has for me. God is love, and I abide in love and I abide in God. God's love is perfected within me. I have confidence for the day of judgement, because as He is, so am I in this world. I have no fear, perfect love has cast it out of me. I am perfected in the love of God. I now love because God first loved me.

"I surrender to His good and perfect will for my life."

Chosen by

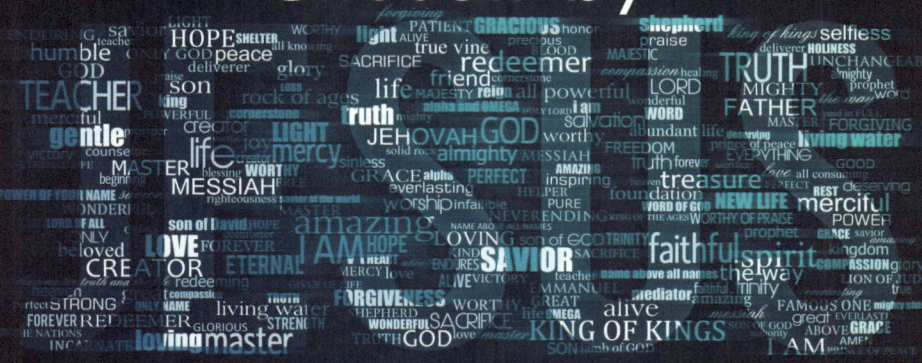

I am His chosen daughter—not forsaken, but redeemed—for such a time as this.

But you are a chosen race, a royal priesthood, a holy nation, a people for his own possession, that you may proclaim the excellencies of him who called you out of darkness into his marvelous light.

-1 Peter 2:9 ESV

Chosen by Jesus

I am a chosen race, a royal priesthood, a holy nation, a people for His own possession. I am proclaiming the excellencies of Him who called me out of darkness into His marvelous light.

Praise be to the God and Father of our Lord Jesus Christ, the Father of compassion and the God of all comfort, who comforts us in all our troubles, so that we can comfort those in any trouble with the comfort we ourselves receive from God.
-2 Corinthians 1:3-4 NIV

Chosen by Jesus

I do hear the voice of God.

My sheep listen to my voice; I know them, and they follow me.
I give them eternal life, and they shall never perish;
no one will snatch them out of my hand.
-John 10:27-28 NIV

Chosen by Jesus

I do hear and am listening for God's voice because I belong to God and He knows my name. I shall never perish but have eternal life in Jesus Christ. Nothing and no one can snatch me out of God's hand. God is watching over me. My heart is attentive to the word of God.

Since you have kept my command to endure patiently, I will also keep you from the hour of trial that is going to come on the whole world to test the inhabitants of the earth. I am coming soon. Hold on to what you have, so that no one will take your crown.
-Revelation 3:10-11 NIV

"I surrender to His good and perfect will for my life."

Chosen by Jesus

I believe in the power of His resurrection.

But if the Spirit of Him who raised Jesus from the dead lives in you,
He who raised Christ from the dead will also give life to your
mortal bodies through His Spirit that lives in you.
-Romans 8:11 MEV

Chosen by Jesus

The same Spirit who raised Jesus from the dead lives in me! Therefore, He who raised Christ from the dead also gives life to my mortal body through His Spirit who lives in me.

Heaven and earth will pass away, but my words will never pass away.
—Matthew 24:35 NIV

Praise, Prayer, & Power

I praise Him in good times and bad times.

I will praise the Lord at all times. I will constantly speak his praises.
—Psalm 34:1 NLT

[G]ive thanks in all circumstances;
for this is God's will for you in Christ Jesus.
—1 Thessalonians 5:18 NIV

Praise, Prayer, & Power

**I praise the Lord at all times, whether good or bad.
I give thanks to the Lord and speak His praises constantly.
I am thankful in all circumstances.
This is God's will for me in Christ Jesus.**

*In the same way, let your light shine before others, that they may
see your good deeds and glorify your Father in heaven.
—Matthew 5:16 NIV*

Praise, Prayer, & Power

I watch and I pray. God hears and He answers.

*This is the confidence we have in approaching God:
that if we ask anything according to his will, he hears us.*
—1 John 5:14 NIV

*In the morning, Lord, you hear my voice; in the morning
I lay my requests before you and wait expectantly.*
—Psalm 5:3 NIV

*For the eyes of the Lord are on the righteous and his ears are attentive
to their prayer, but the face of the Lord is against those who do evil.*
—1 Peter 3:12 NIV

Praise, Prayer, & Power

I watch and I pray. I have confidence that I can approach God. So, every day I lay down my requests before the Lord and wait expectantly. I am the righteousness of God in Christ Jesus. His eyes are upon me. God hears my prayers and answers them according to His will.

Jesus answered,
"It is written: 'Worship the Lord your God and serve him only.'"
—Luke 4:8 NIV

"I surrender to His good and perfect will for my life."

Praise, Prayer, & Power

"The Christ-like spirit is now resulting from the change that has taken place in our spirits during the time we have spent with *The Interactive Healing Devotional for All Women* and the Bible. Forgiveness is KEY to move on to *the* higher place with Jesus and claim victory through endurance and compassion for the afflicted who still carry great pain." - INA

As it is written in the Scriptures:

"And without faith it is impossible to please God..." (Hebrews 11:6). Our relationship with the Lord is totally dependent on it. Faith is what brings the things God has provided for us from the spiritual realm into the physical realm (see Hebrews 11:1). Our faith is the victory that enables us to overcome the world (see 1 John 5:4). Everything the Lord does for us is accessed by grace through faith!

Blessed be the God and Father of our Lord Jesus Christ, the Father of compassion and God of all encouragement, who encourages us in our every affliction, so that we may be able to encourage those who are in any affliction with the encouragement with which we ourselves are encouraged by God. For as Christ's sufferings overflow to us, so through Christ does our encouragement also overflow.
—2 Corinthians 1:3–5 NABRE

Now it's time to be made new by every revelation that's been given to you. And to be transformed as you embrace the glorious Christ-within as your new life and live in union with him! For God has re-created you all over again in his perfect righteousness, and you now belong to him in the realm of true holiness.
—Ephesians 4:23-24 TPT

Praise, Prayer, & Power

Who could ever find a wife like this one — she is a woman of strength and mighty valor! She's full of wealth and wisdom. The price paid for her was greater than many jewels. Her husband has entrusted his heart to her, for she brings him the rich spoils of victory. All throughout her life she brings him what is good and not evil. She searches out continually to possess that which is pure and righteous. She delights in the work of her hands. She gives out revelation-truth to feed others. She is like a trading ship bringing divine supplies from the merchant. Even in the night season she arises and sets food on the table for hungry ones in her house and for others. She sets her heart upon a field and takes it as her own. She labors there to plant the living vines. She wraps herself in strength, might, and power in all her works. She tastes and experiences a better substance, and her shining light will not be extinguished, no matter how dark the night. She stretches out her hands to help the needy and she lays hold of the wheels of government. She is known by her extravagant generosity to the poor, for she always reaches out her hands to those in need. She is not afraid of tribulation, for all her household is covered in the dual garments of righteousness and grace. Her clothing is beautifully knit together — a purple gown of exquisite linen. Her husband is famous and admired by all, sitting as the venerable judge of his people. Even her works of righteousness she does for the benefit of her enemies. Bold power and glorious majesty are wrapped around her as she laughs with joy over the latter days. Her teachings are filled with wisdom and kindness as loving instruction pours from her lips. She watches over the ways of her household and meets every need they have. Her sons and daughters arise in one accord to extol her virtues, and her husband arises to speak of her in glowing terms. "There are many valiant and noble ones, but you have ascended above them all!" Charm can be misleading, and beauty is vain and so quickly fades, but this virtuous woman lives in the wonder, awe, and fear of the Lord. She will be praised throughout eternity. So go ahead and give her the credit that is due, for she has become a radiant woman, and all her loving works of righteousness deserve to be admired at the gateways of every city! 																-Proverbs 31:10-31

Praise, Prayer, & Power

_____
_____
_____
_____
_____
_____
_____
_____
_____
_____
_____
_____
_____
_____
_____
_____
_____
_____
_____
_____
_____
_____
_____
_____
_____
_____
_____
_____
_____
_____
_____
_____
_____
_____
_____
_____
_____
_____

Dance

And so I did.
I danced the
Father Daughter Dance of
Freedom and Redemption

"I surrender to His good and perfect will for my life."

Dance

["]For I know the plans I have for you," declares the Lord, "plans to prosper you and not to harm you, plans to give you hope and a future.["]
—Jeremiah 29:11 NIV

Dance

. . ."Fear not, for I have redeemed you; I have called you by your name; You are Mine. When you pass through the waters, I will be with you; and through the rivers, they shall not overflow you. When you walk through the fire, you shall not be burned, nor shall the flame scorch you. For I am the Lord your God, The Holy One of Israel, your Savior,["]
—Isaiah 43:1-3

Dance

Instead of your shame you will receive a double portion, and instead of disgrace you will rejoice in your inheritance. And so you will inherit a double portion in your land, and everlasting joy will be yours.
—Isaiah 61:7 NIV

Dance

*But they that wait upon the Lord shall renew their strength;
they shall mount up with wings as eagles; they shall run,
and not be weary; and they shall walk, and not faint.
—Isaiah 40:31 KJV*

"I surrender to His good and perfect will for my life."

Dance

LORD JEHOVAH your God within you, The Mighty Man and The Savior, He shall sweeten you in joy and He shall make you new in His love, and He shall make you dance with a song as that in the day of a feast.
—Zephaniah 3:17 ABPE

Dance

The Lord your God wins victory after victory and is always with you. He celebrates and sings because of you, and he will refresh your life with his love.
—Zephaniah 3:17 CEV

"I surrender to His good and perfect will for my life."

Dance

"Ask and it will be given to you; seek and you will find; knock and the door will be opened to you. For everyone who asks receives; the one who seeks finds; and to the one who knocks, the door will be opened."
—Matthew 7:7-8 NIV

Dance

But seek first his kingdom and his righteousness,
and all these things will be given to you as well.
—Matthew 6:33 NIV

Dance

But love your enemies, do good to them, and lend to them without expecting to get anything back. Then your reward will be great, and you will be children of the Most High, because he is kind to the ungrateful and wicked.
—Luke 6:35 NIV

. . . Freely you have received, freely give.
—Matthew 10:8

Dance

For I am the Lord your God who takes hold of your right hand and says to you, Do not fear; I will help you.
—Isaiah 41:13 NIV

He is Risen!

I am Redeemed

I am who You say I am. I have overcome the world by the blood of the Lamb and by the word of my testimony, and I do not love my old life so much that I would be tempted to go back to it (see Revelation 12:11). I am surrendered to the will of God for my life. My life belongs to the Lord. I am no longer in bondage to the fears of this world or the pain that it brings. I am the healed in Christ Jesus. I am free from accusation. I trust the Lord to lead me wherever He wants me to go. My healing bursts forth with rays of glory. I am redeemed from the curse (see Galatians 3:13). I am confident and courageous. I sing praises to the Lord in every season of my life. I forgive and I am forgiven.

My brethren, count it all joy when you fall into various trials, knowing that the testing of your faith produces patience. But let patience have its perfect work, that you may be perfect and complete, lacking nothing.
—James 1:2-4 NKJV

I am free to dance!
I am free to dance with my Father!
I am free!

I am Redeemed

"*For God so loved the world, that he gave his only Son, that whoever believes in him should not perish but have eternal life. For God did not send his Son into the world to condemn the world, but in order that the world might be saved through him.*"
—*John 3:16-17 ESV*

Additional Works

For if you forgive others their trespasses, your heavenly Father will also forgive you, but if you do not forgive others their trespasses, neither will your Father forgive your trespasses.
—Matthew 6:14-15 ESV

Then Peter came up and said to him, "Lord, how often will my brother sin against me, and I forgive him? As many as seven times?" Jesus said to him, *"I do not say to you seven times, but seventy-seven times."*
—Matthew 18:21-22 ESV

And Jesus said,
"Father, forgive them, for they know not what they do." . . .
—Luke 23:34 ESV

Be on the lookout for the Seventy Times Seven Interactive Forgiveness Devotional, another level of freedom in Christ—to add to your collection of the Butterfly Ballerina's Interactive Devotionals for All Women.

Additional Works:

Sought After Author & Speaker

Hardcover, Paperback, & Ebook

DEMONS RELEASE TRILOGIES

THE PREQUEL
BOOK THREE

Liberty Crouch

Liberty's transparency is for other's revival Meet Jesus, the Solution to every plaque, pain, abuse, & pitfall.

Jesus came to seek and to save that which was lost.

Scan below to watch the 700 Club's segment sharing Liberty's story, *Unlocking the Key to Freedom from Addiction.*

Scan below to learn more about the *Demons Release Trilogy:*

Scriptural Index

Scriptural Index

Healing
Acts 5:15-16, pg. 12
Jeremiah 30:17, pg. 27
Acts 3:7-8, pg. 30
Mark 16:18, pg. 34
James 5:14, pg. 34
2 Chronicles 7:14, pg. 56
Ephesians 4:23-24, pg. 69
Revelation 12:11, pg. 83

Help
Hebrews 4:16, pg. 35
Jeremiah 29:12-13, pg. 36
1 Peter 5:7, pgs. 40, 45, & 48
Psalm 18:6, pg. 41
Romans 12:2, pg. 44
James 1:25, pg. 53
John 10:27-28, pg. 61
1 Peter 3:12, pg. 67
Isaiah 40:31, pg. 76
Matthew 7:7-8, pg. 79
Matthew 6:33, pg. 80

Kindness
Proverbs 31:26, pg. i
Jeremiah 31:3-4, pg. 19
Colossians 3:12-17, pg. 50
Matthew 5:16, pg. 66

Love
Matthew 6:21, pg. 18
Jeremiah 31:3-4, pg. 19
Colossians 3:12-17, pg. 50
1 John 4:16-19, pg.
Jeremiah 29:11, pg. 73
Zephaniah 3:17, pgs. 77 & 78
John 3:16-17, pg. 84

Power
2 Corinthians 12:9-10, pg. 13
Luke 4:18-21, pg. 14
Hebrews 4:12, pg. 45
2 Timothy 1:7, pg. 52

Praise
Psalm 7:17, pg. 5
1 Chronicles 16:25, pg. 6
Revelation 5:9-10, pg. 8
Acts 3:7-8, pg. 30
2 Corinthians 1:3-4, pg. 60
Psalm 34:1, pg. 65

Prayer
Matthew 6:6, pg. 40
Psalm 18:6, pg. 41
Romans 8:11, pg. 63

Promise
Numbers 23:19, pg. 20
Jeremiah 30:17, pg. 27
Isaiah 62:2-3, pg. 28
Psalm 145:18, pg. 33
Mark 16:18, pg. 34
James 5:14, pg. 34
Jeremiah 33:3, pg. 34
Matthew 7:7-8, pg. 79
Luke 6:35, pg. 81
Matthew 10:8, pg. 81

Protection
2 Thessalonians 3:3, pg.25
1 Peter 3:12, pg. 67

Purpose
Isaiah 43:7, pg. 2
Revelation 5:9-10, pg. 8
2 Corinthians 4:6-10, pg. 9
Luke 4:18-21, pg. 14
1 Peter 2:9, pg. 59
Psalm 34:1, pg. 65
Jeremiah 29:11, pg. 73

Scriptural Index

www.ingramcontent.com/pod-product-compliance
Lightning Source LLC
Chambersburg PA
CBHW040856120626
46551CB00001B/46